WE SHOCKED THE WORLD

How the underdog St. Louis Cardinals won the 2006 World Series

WE SHOCKED THE WORLD

How the underdog St. Louis Cardinals won the 2006 World Series

Editor
Mike Smith

Art Direction/Design
Wade Wilson

Photo Editor
Larry Coyne

Contributing writers
Joe Strauss, Bryan Burwell, Bernie Miklasz

Assistant photo editor
Hillary Levin

Production coordinator
Bob Rose

Sales and marketing
Gail LaFata, Nancy Long

Special thanks to Doug Weaver
of Kansas City Star Books

ISBN 10 − 0-9661397-7-1
ISBN 13 − 978-0-9661397-7-8

Printed by Walsworth Publishing Co., Marceline, Mo.

To order additional copies, call 800-329-0224.
Order online at www.post-dispatchstore.com

CONTENTS

Survivor: NL Central

THE SCENE • BY JOE STRAUSS

They arrived at the same place by taking a different route, a narrowing path filled with knee-deep potholes, worn shoulders and broken pavement near its end.

But the Cardinals finally reached their destination Oct. 1 in a 5-3 loss to the Milwaukee Brewers. They completed an 83-78 season as National League Central champions on the final day of the regular season because the second-place Houston Astros lost to the Atlanta Braves.

When it was over, a relieved team left its dugout to embrace each other and wave to those left from Busch Stadium's announced crowd of 44,133.

They didn't dominate as they did in their 105-win 2004 season or last year's remarkable 100-win push.

They survived.

The Cardinals' reward for an 83-78 record is their sixth postseason berth and fifth outright division title in seven years.

"It was ugly, but it doesn't matter how you win your division," Albert Pujols said. "We're in it."

It's been this kind of season: The Cardinals accomplished the rare distinction of being booed in the first inning of their clincher.

The final game began with La Russa's "roll of the dice" – starting rookie pitcher Anthony Reyes on three days' rest to preserve ace Chris Carpenter for a hoped-for Game 1 of the playoffs. Reyes lasted only 26 pitches and two outs and left trailing 4-0.

Yet La Russa counted the gamble as a huge victory.

"We're in. We rolled the dice. And we've got Chris Carpenter" to start the playoffs, La Russa said.

"I think our glass is much more full than empty; I don't think it's half and half. But we've had some times when it's been a rough struggle. . . . We could've faded away. But we kept picking ourselves up."

THE VIEW • BY BERNIE MIKLASZ

What a long, strange trip it's been for the 2006 Cardinals. Six months of injuries, insolence, slumps, streaks, fear, fatigue and rallies. The new ballpark seemed like the set of a raucous reality show. The Cardinals gave us 161 games of baseball, and 161 episodes of a story line that twisted and turned up to the final sequence of the regular season.

So on Oct. 1, when the Cardinals finally claimed the National League Central division title, the ending made perfect sense if we consider the bizarro nature of their season. The clinching victory was actually executed by the Atlanta Braves, who eliminated Houston to shoo those annoying Killer Bs away from the Cardinals.

The Cardinals didn't win on the field but won on the out-of-town scoreboard. It's a little confusing. Do we congratulate the Cardinals or give them cold compresses and IV hookups? Will they charter an airplane for the flight to San Diego for the first-round playoff series or be transported on a Medivac helicopter?

With the champagne and Anheuser-Busch products being sprayed and poured in a rowdy clubhouse across the hallway, Cardinals manager Tony La Russa quietly sat in his office, trying to offer perspective. How do you possibly summarize a turbulent six-month sweep of events in a few sentences?

Fatigued by stress and a cold, La Russa coughed repeatedly as he spoke to reporters. But after what he'd been through over the last two weeks, La Russa could handle that. He could handle just about anything now. The manager could clear out his chest and lungs for hours if he had to. Because La Russa's team did not choke. That's what really matters.

Anthony Reyes reacts to a two-run homer by Milwaukee's Prince Fielder on the final day of the regular season. Although Reyes is ineffective, the Cardinals' gamble in starting him pays off because it makes a rested Chris Carpenter available for the first game of the playoffs.

ABOVE: Despite trailing 5-0 in the bottom of the sixth, Preston Wilson beams after learning the Cardinals have clinched the division title.

LEFT: Scott Spiezio celebrates the Cardinals' three-homer barrage in the bottom of the ninth. Although the Cardinals drop the game, the offense is tuning up for the playoffs.

After clinching the division title with a loss, manager Tony La Russa is weary but optimistic.."We'll be a dangerous club in the playoffs," he predicts.

John Rodriguez is showered with a combination of champagne and beer as the Cardinals celebrate their third consecutive National League Central title and sixth trip to the playoffs in seven seasons.

Broadway bound

THE SCENE • BY JOE STRAUSS

A team built around large, expensive and at times ill-fitting pieces came together to form a functional mosaic Oct. 8 at Busch Stadium. Its Game 4 glue came from parts unknown, or at least places no one could have guessed six months or even six weeks ago.

Confronted with the unpleasant possibility of a flight to the West Coast to play a decisive game, the Cardinals overcame a first-inning pratfall by their signature starting pitcher to secure a 6-2 win over the San Diego Padres, and with it their third first-round series in as many years.

The Cardinals will open the National League Championship Series in New York against the Mets because:
• Ronnie Belliard, a second baseman found for the season's first four months in Cleveland, granted them a first-inning tie following a jarring start to the night.
• April's Invisible Man, Juan Encarnacion, provided the game-winning RBI on an opposite-field triple.
• Scott Spiezio, a player raised from Seattle's career dead, gave them a two-run cushion.
• Josh Kinney, a former River City Rascal and now a 27-year-old rookie, pulled off an eighth-inning escape.
• A pitcher unable to make the team's April starting rotation, Adam Wainwright, found himself the obvious choice to throw the clincher's final pitch.

"You almost expected we'd have to go back (to San Diego) because that's the way our season has gone," manager Tony La Russa said. "But what these guys did tonight, this series, was nothing short of remarkable -- all of them."

Spiezio said: "Every team that wins needs guys who aren't expected to come up big in the clutch. You look at what's happened here, that's what it is."

THE VIEW • BY BERNIE MIKLASZ

All but counted out in the final days of September, the Cardinals had the audacity to survive and advance into the next round of October. With the Yankees, Twins, Dodgers and Padres already fallen, the Cardinals are still standing, still defiantly pouring champagne into their open wounds.

Suddenly it's a red October, an October of redemption. And it wasn't supposed to happen this way. The Cardinals entered the postseason with the fewest wins and the most scars. As St. Louis staggered into the National League Division Series and the optimistic atmosphere set by the hopeful Padres and their fans in San Diego, Cardinal red looked like the color of fresh bloodstains. Soon the bedraggled Cardinals would be put out of their misery. Three and out.

"It's fun to be an underdog for a change," Cardinals chairman Bill DeWitt said after his franchise booked passage to New York and the NL Championship Series with a 6-2 clincher over the Padres in Game 4 of the NLDS. "The last couple of seasons, we were expected to win. That can be a difficult role. It might be more fun this way."

The Cardinals are more intriguing, more mysterious, than ever as they prepare to engage the New York Mets. Maybe this NLDS did nothing for the Cardinals but serve them up as an easy mark, a hapless victim, for the powerful Mets and the howling mob at Shea Stadium. The Cardinals will be heavy underdogs again, but as DeWitt suggests, that's a plus.

When you are a team that lost nearly everything, finding the way back can take you to places you'd never dreamed of. Remember the old Kris Kristofferson lyric: Freedom's just another word for nothing left to lose.

The turning point of Game 1: Padres catcher Mike Piazza crashes against the net behind the plate as he misses a pop foul by Albert Pujols in the fourth inning. With a second chance, Pujols hits a two-run homer to start the scoring.

Yadier Molina throws to first to retire Padres center fielder Dave Roberts in Game 4. Molina's arm neutralizes opposing baserunners throughout the entire postseason.

Ronnie Belliard gets a hand from coach Dave McKay after his two-run hit in the first ties Game 4. The inning ends when Belliard slips between first and second base and is tagged out.

Scott Spiezio lashes a run-scoring single past Cla Meredith in the sixth inning of Game 4. Spiezio is in the lineup to replace third baseman Scott Rolen, who is battling a sore shoulder.

Cardinals fans and players toast each other on another trip to the League Championship Series. Even Jose Vizcaino, who isn't on the postseason roster, joins in the celebration.

KEY MOMENTS

GAME ONE • SAN DIEGO

Cardinals 5, Padres 1

After Padres catcher Mike Piazza flubs a pop foul by Albert Pujols in a scoreless game, Pujols connects for a two-run homer.

WP • Carpenter
LP • Peavy
HR • Pujols (STL)

GAME TWO • SAN DIEGO

Cardinals 2, Padres 0

After five scoreless innings by Jeff Weaver, Cards bullpen gets the final 12 outs, striking out six and allowing just three base runners.

WP • Weaver
LP • Wells
SAVE • Wainwright

GAME THREE • ST. LOUIS

Padres 3, Cardinals 1

In the fourth inning of a scoreless game, Russell Branyan ropes a two-run double to the right-field corner to give San Diego its first lead over the Cardinals in a playoff game in a decade.

WP • Young
LP • Suppan
SAVE • Hoffman
HR • Taguchi (STL)

GAME FOUR • ST. LOUIS

Cardinals 6, Padres 2

Juan Encarnacion lashes a triple to the right-field corner to bring in Albert Pujols and break a 2-2 tie in the sixth. The Cards score three more in the sixth, capped by David Eckstein's RBI on a suicide squeeze.

WP • Carpenter
LP • Williams

Tony La Russa dons some unusual headgear to seek shelter from the spray of champagne during the clubhouse celebration. John Rodriguez offers his manager little protection.

Unlikely heroes

THE SCENE • BY JOE STRAUSS

The ball kept climbing, then hanging and, finally, it fell. And when it landed a dozen or so feet beyond Shea Stadium's left-field wall with one out in the ninth inning of Game 7, Yadier Molina's six months of struggle magically transformed into an indelible marker within an increasingly improbable season.

Molina, a precocious defensive talent often left to feel self-conscious about his hitting, shoved the Cardinals into their 17th World Series by turning New York Mets righthanded reliever Aaron Heilman's breaking ball into a two-run home run. The blast snapped a 1-1 tie and gave the Cardinals a 3-1 lead that nervous rookie closer Adam Wainwright clung to for the franchise's second pennant in three years.

"It stayed there a long time. I didn't know where it was coming down," Molina said. "When it came down, I just looked into my dugout and saw everybody jumping up and down screaming. It's the best feeling I've ever had."

"I just prayed," Molina said. "I prayed Endy Chavez wouldn't catch the ball."

Chavez, the Mets' left fielder, had denied the Cardinals a 3-1 lead in the sixth inning when he reached over the same wall to steal a two-run homer from Scott Rolen. Against Molina, however, Chavez could only retreat, look up and stare at an advertising slogan proclaiming "The Strength To Be There."

Wainwright survived consecutive singles to begin the ninth and a bases-loading two-out walk by striking out nemesis Carlos Beltran on three pitches. The third, a sharp curve, froze Beltran for a called strike.

"I'm not a guy who gets nervous. I can remember only a handful of times in my life when I've been really nervous. This was the most nervous I've ever been in my life," Wainwright said.

THE VIEW • BY BRYAN BURWELL

Your nerves were in a blender. Your stomach was doing back flips. Your heart felt like some reverberating bass speakers at a hip-hop concert. The deeper the Cardinals and New York Mets traveled into this rainy night, the emotions of the most important night of the National League season twisted tighter than a tourniquet.

So what does a Game 7 feel like? Just like this, frightening and delightful. Maddening and joyful. Frustrating and breathless all rolled into one. It feels like a crazy, improbable journey that makes no sense at all, and at the same time makes all the sense in the world.

Just around midnight in the city that never sleeps, shocked Mets fans spilled into the Shea Stadium parking lot, which was filled with a disappointed mix of raindrops and tear drops. The Mets — the best team in the National League — had been eliminated from the National League Championship Series, and none of these hard-bitten New Yorkers could figure out how.

All they needed to do was eavesdrop in on the visitors' clubhouse, which was soaked with a pungent spray of cheap champagne, beer and Gatorade. Inside the Cardinals' clubhouse there were plenty of answers for what had just transpired.

Cardinals 3, Mets 1. See ya later, New York. Hello, Detroit, St. Louis calling.

It makes no sense how the improbable underdog Redbirds are on their way to the World Series after winning the NLCS in one of the most dramatic Game 7s in memory. It makes no sense, but it's clear as a bell.

What does a Game 7 feel like?

"It's feels unbelievable!" second baseman Ronnie Belliard shouted.

So Taguchi is congratulated by teammates after he hits the game-winning home run in the ninth inning of Game 2. Taguchi's shot off reliever Billy Wagner silences the Shea Stadium crowd.

Jeff Suppan cements his reputation as a big-game pitcher by limiting the Mets to one run in Game 7. That performance, along with his scoreless effort in Game 3, earns him the series MVP honors.

KEY MOMENTS

GAME ONE • NEW YORK

Mets 2, Cardinals 0

After five-plus innings of one-hit pitching, Jeff Weaver allows a two-out single to Paul LoDuca. Carlos Beltran slams a 2-2 pitch off the right-field scoreboard for the only runs of the game.

WP • Glavine **LP** • Weaver
SAVE • Wagner **HR** • Beltran (NY)

GAME TWO • NEW YORK

Cardinals 9, Mets 6

After overcoming 3-0 and 6-4 deficits, the Cardinals face Billy Wagner in the top of the ninth. So Taguchi, who had entered the game as a defensive replacement, falls behind 0-2 before hitting a 3-2 pitch over the left-field wall for the Cardinals' first lead of the series.

WP • Kinney **LP** • Wagner **HR** • Edmonds (STL); Taguchi (STL); Delgado 2 (NY)

GAME THREE • ST. LOUIS

Cardinals 5, Mets 0

Jeff Suppan holds the Mets to three hits in eight innings and allows only two of them to get in scoring position. Suppan gets 90 feet farther than any Met does against him when he hits a solo homer to lead off the second.

WP • Suppan **LP** • Trachsel **HR** • Suppan (STL)

GAME FOUR • ST. LOUIS

Mets 12, Cardinals 5

With the game tied 2-2, Brad Thompson replaces Anthony Reyes in the top of the fifth. Two Mets reach base ahead of Carlos Delgado, who homers into the left-field bullpen. The Mets settle this one with six runs in the top of the sixth.

WP • Perez **LP** • Thompson **HR** • Beltran (NY), Delgado (NY), Wright (NY), Edmonds (STL), Eckstein (STL), Molina (STL)

GAME FIVE • ST. LOUIS

Cardinals 4, Mets 2

Jeff Weaver battles through six innings, allowing just two runs as the Mets go one for eight with runners in scoring position. Late-season acquisitions Ronnie Belliard and Preston Wilson drive in the tying and go-ahead runs.

WP • Weaver **LP** • Glavine
SAVE • Wainwright **HR** • Duncan (STL), Pujols (STL)

GAME SIX • NEW YORK

Mets 4, Cardinals 2

John Maine's night isn't pretty, but it's effective. He pitches 5 $\frac{1}{3}$ innings — one inning longer than his previous playoff best — and works around four walks in outdueling Chris Carpenter.

WP • Maine **LP** • Carpenter **HR** • Reyes (NY)

GAME SEVEN • NEW YORK

Cardinals 3, Mets 1

Yadier Molina punctuates a brilliant series with a decisive two-run homer in the top of the ninth. He also shepherds series MVP Jeff Suppan through a Game 7 gem (seven innings, two hits) and rookie closer Adam Wainwright through a harrowing bottom of the ninth.

WP • Flores **LP** • Heilman **HR** • Molina (STL) **SAVE** • Wainwright

RIGHT • Endy Chavez robs Scott Rolen of a home run in the sixth inning of Game 7.

The shot heard 'round New York ... and St. Louis ... and the baseball world: Yadier Molina follows the ninth-inning home run that vaults him into Cardinals history and his team into the World Series.

Molina leaps for joy after Adam Wainwright fans Carlos Beltran with the bases loaded for the final out of Game 7.

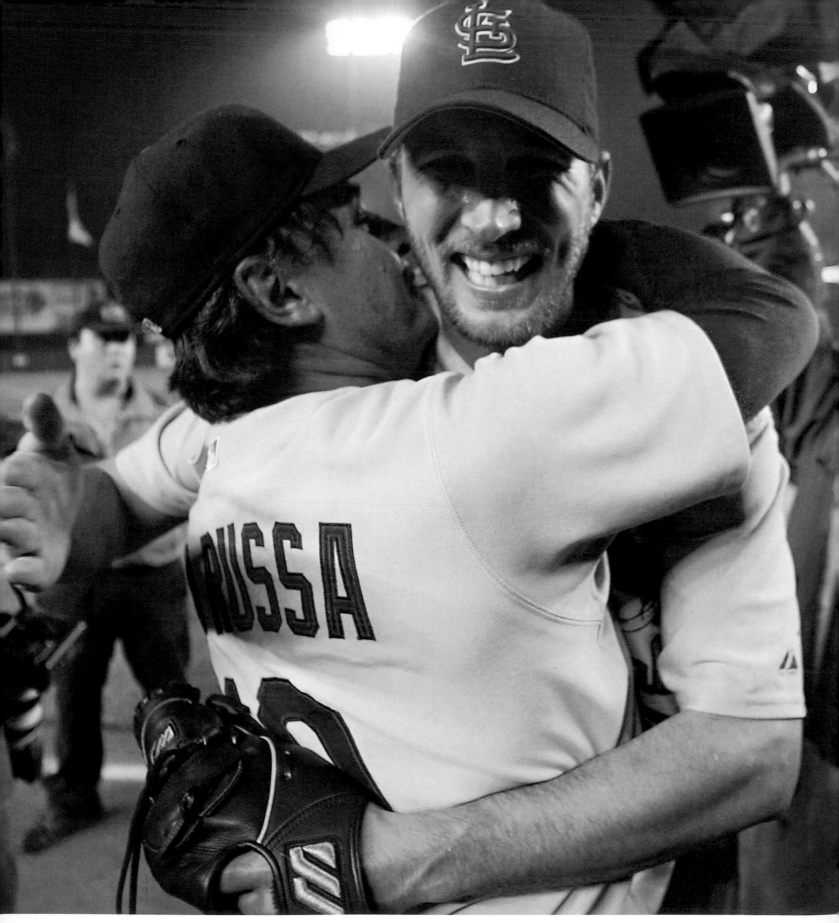

Tony La Russa celebrates the pennant-winning victory with his new closer, Adam Wainwright. An injury to Jason Isringhausen late in the regular season leads to a reshuffling of the Cardinals bullpen, with Wainwright emerging as the main man.

Mowdown in Motown

THE SCENE • BY JOE STRAUSS

Until Oct. 21 at Comerica Park, Anthony Reyes was mostly known as Mark Prior's college teammate, the Cardinals' rookie fifth starter, the guy with the flat hat who might turn into a pumpkin after the sixth inning.

When he left the mound one pitch into the ninth inning, Reyes had altered the look of a World Series that he entered as a last-minute opening act.

Reyes' unbreakable performance lasted eight-plus innings and pushed the Cardinals to a 7-2 win over the Detroit Tigers in Game 1.

"Winning the game tonight gives us a fighting chance to win the whole thing. We know they are capable of winning four of the next six, but we certainly think we're capable of winning three of the next six," said manager Tony La Russa. The Cardinals won their first Series game since Oct. 22, 1987.

A first-inning home run by Scott Rolen, designated hitter Chris Duncan's go-ahead double in the third and first baseman Albert Pujols' two-out, two-run homer in the same inning gave Reyes a lead he wouldn't give up.

"He's a rookie and he's going into his first World Series," La Russa said. "As far as challenges go, that's a little unfair."

La Russa had asked his coaching staff to write down its predictions of what Reyes would do. No one wrote down fewer than five innings, but bullpen catcher Jeff Murphy called the shot by guessing eight innings and two runs.

"They said stay ready for the postseason because you never know what happens, and I did," Reyes said. "It worked out pretty nice for me."

THE VIEW • BY BERNIE MIKLASZ

If, for some reason, he channel-surfed on Oct. 21 in his office at Comerica Park, Cardinals manager Tony La Russa may have come across a replay of Game 1 of the 1988 World Series on ESPN Classic.

That was the Kirk Gibson Game. Powered by will, the limping Gibson smashed the winning homer off Dennis Eckersley to carry the Los Angeles Dodgers over La Russa's universally favored Oakland A's. Oakland never recovered from the shock.

That game came to define La Russa's hideously cruel fate in the Fall Classic. Yes, Oakland swept San Francisco in 1989, but in three other World Series, La Russa teams went 0-3 and were humiliated in losing 12 of 13 games. That includes Boston's merciless four-game sweep of the Cardinals in 2004.

Maybe the bad karma has changed for La Russa. Perhaps the reversal was set in motion when Yadier Molina had a Gibson moment, homering in the ninth inning to Taser the New York Mets in an epic Game 7 of the National League Championship Series.

The season of the switch continued in Game 1 of the 2006 World Series, with La Russa's Cardinals feeding another set of predictions through the shredder during a 7-2 victory over the Detroit Tigers.

It was La Russa's first win in a World Series game since Oct. 28, 1989. That is not a misprint; until Game 1 in Motown, one of the game's most heralded and respected managers hadn't won a World Series contest in nearly 17 years. La Russa plays it down, but this glaring failure mortified a proud man.

"I never thought about that at all," La Russa said after Game 1. He rolled his eyes to make sure that the interviewer knew how much the losing bothered him.

"But this isn't a personal thing for me. I refuse to look at it that way," he said. "It feels good, because the last time we were in this, we got beat four in a row."

Jim Leyland and Tony La Russa square off in the 2006 World Series as close friends and two of the most respected managers in the game.

KEY MOMENTS

Detroit manager Jim Leyland promised himself not to let Cardinals slugger Albert Pujols beat his team. But three innings into the Series, he got burned when Tigers starter Justin Verlander attacked Pujols with two outs and first base open.

Pujols rode a high fastball for a two-run homer to right field and a 4-1 Cardinals lead.

"I pitched to him and he obviously burned us," Leyland said. "I'm not going to get into a lot of explanation about what the thinking was, but I take the bullet there."

After Pujols' homer sailed into the seats, Verlander gave catcher Pudge Rodriguez an incredulous look.

"It wasn't a bad pitch to most people, but it was to him," Verlander said. "Obviously, he's one of the best hitters in the game, and he'll take advantage of even the littlest mistake. I missed by an inch, and he hurts me for it."

RIGHT: Rookie pitcher Anthony Reyes surrenders a run in the first and a run in the ninth, but that's all he allows the Tigers.

Home plate umpire Randy Marsh signals Scott Rolen safe at home, not because he beats the tag, but because Tigers third baseman Brandon Inge interferes with him during the sixth-inning play. Rolen regains his stroke in Game 1, hitting a home run and a double.

First base coach Dave McKay directs Albert Pujols toward second after Justin Verlander's pickoff throw eludes Carlos Guillen. Pujols moves to third on the play and later scores on a single by Jim Edmonds.

GAME 1 FINAL	1	2	3	4	5	6	7	8	9	R	H	E
ST. LOUIS <<	0	1	3	0	0	3	0	0	0	7	8	2
DETROIT	1	0	0	0	0	0	0	0	1	2	4	3

ST. LOUIS CARDINALS

HITTERS	AB	R	H	RBI	BB	SO	AVG
David Eckstein, SS	5	0	0	0	0	1	.174
Chris Duncan, DH	4	1	1	1	0	2	.167
a- Preston Wilson, PH-DH	1	0	0	0	0	1	.192
Albert Pujols, 1B	3	2	1	2	1	1	.325
Jim Edmonds, CF	4	1	2	1	0	2	.282
Scott Rolen, 3B	4	2	2	1	0	1	.222
Juan Encarnacion, RF	3	0	0	1	1	0	.205
Ronnie Belliard, 2B	4	0	0	0	0	1	.286
Yadier Molina, C	4	1	1	0	0	1	.325
So Taguchi, LF	4	0	1	0	0	0	.625
Totals	**36**	**7**	**8**	**6**	**2**	**10**	

a-struck out for Duncan in the 9th

PITCHERS	IP	H	R	ER	BB	SO	ERA
Anthony Reyes (W,1-0)	8	4	2	2	1	4	3.00
Braden Looper	1	0	0	0	0	1	3.68

BATTING
2B • Chris Duncan (1, Verlander), Scott Rolen (3, Verlander)
HR • Albert Pujols (3, Verlander), Scott Rolen (1, Verlander)
RBI • Chris Duncan (2), Albert Pujols 2 (6), Jim Edmonds (7), Scott Rolen (1), Juan Encarnacion (5)
2-out RBI • Chris Duncan (1), Albert Pujols 2 (2)
Team LOB • 4

FIELDING
E • Juan Encarnacion (1, Misplayed grounder), Scott Rolen (3, Misplayed grounder)

PITCHING
PITCHES-STRIKES • Anthony Reyes 87-63, Braden Looper 22-15
GROUND BALLS-FLY BALLS • Anthony Reyes 3-17, Braden Looper 2-1
BATTERS FACED • Anthony Reyes 29, Braden Looper 4

DETROIT TIGERS

HITTERS	AB	R	H	RBI	BB	SO	AVG
Curtis Granderson, CF	4	0	0	0	0	0	.278
Craig Monroe, LF	4	2	2	1	0	0	.324
Placido Polanco, 2B	4	0	0	0	0	0	.421
Magglio Ordonez, RF	3	0	0	0	1	1	.229
Carlos Guillen, 1B	4	0	2	1	0	1	.382
Ivan Rodriguez, C	4	0	0	0	0	0	.152
Sean Casey, DH	3	0	0	0	0	1	.304
Brandon Inge, 3B	3	0	0	0	0	1	.200
Ramon Santiago, SS	2	0	0	0	0	1	.000
a- Marcus Thames, PH	1	0	0	0	0	0	.238
Neifi Perez, SS	0	0	0	0	0	0	.000
Totals	**32**	**2**	**4**	**2**	**1**	**5**	

a-popped out for Santiago in the 8th

PITCHERS	IP	H	R	ER	BB	SO	ERA
Justin Verlander (L,1-1)	5	6	7	6	2	8	7.47
Jason Grilli	1	0	0	0	0	0	0.00
Fernando Rodney	1	0	0	0	0	1	0.00
Wil Ledezma	1	1	0	0	0	0	2.45
Todd Jones	0.2	1	0	0	0	0	0.00
Jamie Walker	0.1	0	0	0	0	1	4.15

BATTING
2B • Craig Monroe (4, An. Reyes)
HR • Craig Monroe (4, An. Reyes)
RBI • Craig Monroe (8), Carlos Guillen (3)
2-out RBI • Carlos Guillen (1)
Team LOB • 4

FIELDING
DP • Polanco-Santiago-Guillen
E • Brandon Inge 2 (2, Throwing), Justin Verlander (1, Throwing)

PITCHING
WP • Jamie Walker (1)
PITCHES-STRIKES • Justin Verlander 96-59, Jason Grilli 11-7, Fernando Rodney 12-10, Wil Ledezma 15-9, Todd Jones 8-7, Jamie Walker 7-4
GROUND BALLS-FLY BALLS • Justin Verlander 6-1, Jason Grilli 2-2, Wil Ledezma 1-2, Todd Jones 2-0
BATTERS FACED • Justin Verlander 23, Jason Grilli 4, Fernando Rodney 3, Wil Ledezma 4, Todd Jones 3, Jamie Walker 1

Batting and earned-run averages are cumulative for postseason

GAME INFORMATION
Attendance • 42,479
Game time • 2:54
Temperature • 56

UMPIRES
Home • Randy Marsh
1st base • Alfonso Marquez
2nd base • Wally Bell
3rd base • Mike Winters
Left field • John Hirschbeck
Right field • Tim McClelland

HOW THEY SCORED

Tigers first inning • With one out, Monroe doubled to left. With two outs, Guillen singled to right, Monroe scored • One run
Tigers 1, Cardinals 0

Cardinals second inning • With one out, Rolen homered to left • One run
Cardinals 1, Tigers 1.

Cardinals third inning • Molina singled to right. Taguchi grounded out, Molina to second. With two outs, Duncan doubled to right, Molina scored. Pujols homered to right, Duncan scored • Three runs
Cardinals 4, Tigers 1

Cardinals sixth inning • Pujols walked. On Verlander's error on a pickoff attempt, Pujols to third. Edmonds singled to right, Pujols scored. Rolen doubled to right, Edmonds to third. Encarnacion safe on fielder's choice and Inge's error, Edmonds scored, Rolen to third. On Inge's error, Rolen scored • Three runs
Cardinals 7, Tigers 1

Tigers ninth inning • Monroe homered to left • One run
Final score
Cardinals 7, Tigers 2

Under his thumb

THE SCENE • BY JOE STRAUSS

Kenny Rogers once lived under the shadow of a pitcher who did his best work early in the season before wilting late and ultimately folding in October. That pitcher was nowhere to be found Oct. 22 at Comerica Park.

The Detroit Tigers' lefthander invited some first-inning intrigue, then followed with seven innings of dominance as Rogers pushed the American League champions to a 3-1 win in Game 2.

Did Rogers beat them with a remote-control sinker or an accelerated fastball? Or, as the Cardinals wondered during the first inning, was the veteran working with something "extra?"

"It's not important to talk about," Cardinals manager Tony La Russa said. "I thought he pitched very well. I thought we hit the ball better than two hits. I don't think we hit well enough to get more than three runs."

The Cardinals managed only two hits off Rogers, who at 41 years, 11 months, 12 days became the oldest pitcher ever to win a postseason game.

They also made a first-inning inquiry to the umpiring crew about what was on Rogers' left thumb.

A mini-controversy that began when Fox TV showed Rogers' discolored thumb led to suggestions that he was pitching with a tacky substance to help his feel for the ball on a windy night with temperatures in the mid-40s. Rogers and the umpires said it was dirt.

"I went in to look at my first at-bat and the guys in the clubhouse had a still frame" of Rogers' pitching hand, said designated hitter Scott Spiezio.

"Somebody said they saw pine tar on it. That's about it. He obviously got rid of it or he never had it in the first place," said second baseman Aaron Miles. "The stuff looked about the same as it did at the beginning. I'm not sure what difference it made."

THE VIEW • BY BRYAN BURWELL

As the Cardinals slipped out of Comerica Park with one surprising World Series victory already in their hip pockets, it's as good a time as any to put the events of this frostbitten weekend in Motown into their proper perspective.

The makings of an improbable World Series upset have already been put into motion. The Detroit Tigers may have defeated the Redbirds 3-1 to tie this best-of-seven series at 1-1. But the American League champs ought to be staggering out of town with huge lumps in their throats and a queasy feeling in their guts, because this series that was supposed to be a perfunctory detail in Detroit's date with World Series destiny has suddenly turned into a real tussle.

"Well, I'm not unhappy," said Cardinals manager Tony La Russa following the Game 2 loss to 41-year-old Tiger ace Kenny Rogers. "I felt like for two days we've come in here and competed really well. I feel like we're competing the way we did all October, and if we continue to do that, we have a real shot."

Right now, I know what you're thinking.

You want blood. You want Kenny Rogers and his dirty thumb hoisted on piano wire from the top of the Gateway Arch. You think the man cheated his way to that Game 2 victory with an illegal pomade of something that likely involves some weird mixture of dirt, pine tar, cat tails, rat guts and the oily secretions from the intestines of 12 dead pigeons.

But no one attempted to nail Kenny Rogers. The umps didn't slam him up against the dugout wall. They didn't call in CSI: Detroit to swab him down or get DNA samples. They not only didn't accuse him of cheating, they let him go back out there and baffle the Cardinals for the rest of the night, and the worst thing they did to him was make him wash his hands.

Dirt or pine tar? A detail of the pitching hand of Kenny Rogers shows a mysterious discoloration under his thumb. The same discoloration is found in his other two playoff starts, in which he does not yield a run.

KEY MOMENTS

Winning for the third time in as many starts this postseason, Kenny Rogers was good enough in Game 2 to make the Tigers' two-run first inning against Cardinals starting pitcher Jeff Weaver stand up.

Left fielder Craig Monroe hit Weaver's seventh pitch for a home run before first baseman Carlos Guillen's two-out double scored right fielder Magglio Ordonez.

Guillen had three hits and was involved in the Tigers' final two runs, which proved essential as the Cardinals mustered a ninth-inning threat.

Guillen came a home run shy of hitting for the cycle.

RIGHT: Cardinals manager Tony La Russa talks with crew chief Randy Marsh before the second inning, when Kenny Rogers appears with a clean thumb.

FAR RIGHT: Umpire Alfonso Marquez talks to Rogers after the second inning. Rogers later says the conversation is about his warm-up pitches. The supervisor of umpires says it is about his dirty thumb.

ABOVE: Cardinals pitcher Jeff Weaver allows only three runs, but he is consistently in trouble during his five innings of work.
RIGHT: Detroit Tigers third baseman Brandon Inge (15) and Carlos Guillen celebrate the Game 2 victory.

GAME 2 FINAL	1	2	3	4	5	6	7	8	9	R	H	E
ST. LOUIS	0	0	0	0	0	0	0	0	1	1	4	1
DETROIT <<	2	0	0	0	1	0	0	0	x	3	10	0

ST. LOUIS CARDINALS

HITTERS	AB	R	H	RBI	BB	SO	AVG
David Eckstein, SS	4	0	0	0	0	0	.160
Scott Spiezio, DH	3	0	0	0	1	1	.200
Albert Pujols, 1B	3	0	0	0	1	0	.302
Scott Rolen, 3B	4	1	2	0	0	1	.250
Juan Encarnacion, RF	4	0	0	0	0	1	.186
Jim Edmonds, CF	3	0	1	1	1	1	.286
Preston Wilson, LF	3	0	0	0	0	0	.172
Yadier Molina, C	4	0	1	0	0	0	.318
Aaron Miles, 2B	3	0	0	0	0	1	.375
Totals	**31**	**1**	**4**	**1**	**3**	**5**	

PITCHERS	IP	H	R	ER	BB	SO	ERA
Jeff Weaver (L,2-2)	5	9	3	3	1	5	2.91
Tyler Johnson	0.2	0	0	0	0	1	1.29
Josh Kinney	0.1	0	0	0	1	0	0.00
Randy Flores	1	1	0	0	0	0	0.00
Brad Thompson	0.2	0	0	0	0	1	9.00
Adam Wainwright	0.1	0	0	0	0	1	0.00

BATTING

2B • Jim Edmonds (1, T. Jones)
RBI • Jim Edmonds (8)

FIELDING

DP • Miles-Eckstein-Pujols, Rolen-Miles-Pujols
E • Albert Pujols (1, Misplayed grounder)

PITCHING

HBP • Casey (by Jeff Weaver), Polanco (by Josh Kinney)
PITCHES-STRIKES • Jeff Weaver 85-59, Tyler Johnson 9-6, Josh Kinney 8-2, Randy Flores 12-9, Brad Thompson 8-6, Adam Wainwright 5-3
GROUND BALLS-FLY BALLS • Jeff Weaver 7-3, Tyler Johnson 1-0, Randy Flores 1-1, Brad Thompson 1-0
BATTERS FACED • Jeff Weaver 26, Tyler Johnson 2, Josh Kinney 3, Randy Flores 3, Brad Thompson 2, Adam Wainwright 1

DETROIT TIGERS

HITTERS	AB	R	H	RBI	BB	SO	AVG
Curtis Granderson, CF	5	0	0	0	0	2	.244
Craig Monroe, LF	3	1	1	1	1	1	.324
Placido Polanco, 2B	3	0	0	0	0	1	.390
Magglio Ordonez, RF	4	1	2	0	0	0	.256
Carlos Guillen, 1B	3	1	3	1	1	0	.432
Ivan Rodriguez, C	4	0	0	0	0	1	.135
Sean Casey, DH	3	0	1	1	0	0	.308
Brandon Inge, 3B	4	0	2	0	0	2	.235
Ramon Santiago, SS	3	0	1	0	0	1	.083
Totals	**32**	**3**	**10**	**3**	**2**	**8**	

PITCHERS	IP	H	R	ER	BB	SO	ERA
Kenny Rogers (W,3-0)	8	2	0	0	3	5	0.00
Todd Jones (S,4)	1	2	1	0	0	0	0.00

BATTING

2B • Carlos Guillen (5, Weaver)
3B • Carlos Guillen (1, Weaver)
HR • Craig Monroe (5, Weaver)
SH • Ramon Santiago (1)
RBI • Craig Monroe (9), Carlos Guillen (4), Sean Casey (5)

FIELDING

DP • Polanco-Santiago-Guillen
E • Todd Jones (1, Misplayed grounder)

PITCHING

HBP • Pr. Wilson (by Todd Jones)
PITCHES-STRIKES • Kenny Rogers 99-62, Todd Jones 15-10
GROUND BALLS-FLY BALLS • Kenny Rogers 10-8, Todd Jones 3-1
BATTERS FACED • Kenny Rogers 28, Todd Jones 7

Batting and earned-run averages are cumulative for postseason

GAME INFORMATION
Attendance • 42,533
Game time • 2:55
Temperature • 44

UMPIRES
Home • Alfonso Marquez
1st base • Wally Bell
2nd base • Mike Winters

3rd base • John Hirschbeck
Left field • Tim McClelland
Right field • Randy Marsh

HOW THEY SCORED

Tigers first inning • With one out, Monroe homered to left. With two outs, Ordonez singled and scored on Guillen's double to left • Two runs
Tigers 2, Cardinals 0

Tigers fifth inning • With one out, Guillen tripled to right. With two outs, Casey singled to right, Guillen scoring • One run
Tigers 3, Cardinals 0

Cardinals ninth inning • With two outs, Rolen singled. He advanced to second on defensive indifference, and to third when Encarnacion reached on an error. Edmonds doubled to left, Rolen scoring • One run
Final score
Tigers 3, Cardinals 1

Oh, Sweet Heaven!
Thank you Cardinals, for bringing a victorious World Series
to your hometown fans. You gave us more than great stories –
you opened the gates of Baseball Heaven for all the world to see.
Congratulations, Champions!

Untouchable

THE SCENE • BY BERNIE MIKLASZ

On a cold Tuesday night in middle America, a rugged son of New Hampshire took the mound and warmed up Busch Stadium by turning the Tigers' bats into a stack of firewood.

Chris Carpenter was relentless. No, this wasn't Bob Gibson in Game 1 of the 1968 World Series, wiping out 17 Detroit Tigers with a vicious assault of strikeouts. Carpenter's performance in Game 3 of the World Series wouldn't qualify as epic, and the classic-sports TV channel won't be showing black-and-white replays of it 40 years from now. But Carpenter was virtually untouchable, charging through eight shutout innings and leading the Cardinals to a 5-0 victory.

Gibson would be proud of Carpenter. And Carpenter, the Cardinals' most dominant righthanded starter since Gibby, did his best to live up to the glorious tradition, and the high standard, established by the one and only No. 45. The competitive fire that burned inside of Gibson lives on as a flame within Carpenter. Don't let Carpenter's quiet, deep voice and gentle off-field demeanor fool you; he's as nasty as it gets on the mound. Until Tuesday, the Tigers had not been shut out in a World Series game since Gibson's 4-0 masterpiece in 1968.

With Carpenter holding the Tigers by the throat until his teammates could scratch out a few runs, the Cardinals took a 2-1 Series lead, and if this refrigerated Series goes the distance, Carp would get the ball in Game 7. The Tigers may have seen enough. They probably don't want to see him again, looking up as the 6-foot-6 Carpenter glares down at them, the glint of his blue eyes flashing like the blade of a knife.

"Our club comes to the park the day he pitches, and everybody has a real positive expectation," manager Tony La Russa said. "So that's a heck of a burden for the No. 1 guy. When he carries it like he does, everyone feeds off it. So there's a true No. 1."

THE VIEW • BY BRYAN BURWELL

Somebody remind me again just how long ago it was when these Cardinals were gasping and swooning toward the NL Central finish line like punch-drunk boxers just looking for a comfortable place to collapse.

Two weeks? A month?

How about a wild and unbelievable lifetime ago?

The unforeseen road of the Cardinals from unloved regular-season stumblebums to surprising postseason underdogs has just taken another surprising turn with a Game 3 victory over the Detroit Cheatahs ... er ... Tigers. The charmed-life Redbirds have now traveled into one of the oddest, most astonishing destinations of this crazy, mixed-up season.

Say this slowly: The Cardinals really are the favorites in the World Series.

"I think if you've been listening to my press conferences, I've said all along that these guys are pretty good," Tigers manager Jim Leyland said.

A few days ago, it sounded like so much clever posturing from a manager trying to shift the burden off the shoulders of his ballclub. The Tigers came into the World Series justifiably believing they were supposed to be the stars of The Greatest Baseball Story Ever Told (version 2.6). Yet as we traveled deeper and deeper into this chilly night, who among us hasn't begun to reconsider the validity of Leyland's words and contemplate who really does deserve top billing?

It's still too early to be popping champagne corks, charting parade routes and clearing trophy case space. But as 46,513 towel-waving red-clad crazies rose to their feet, and fireworks exploded at the conclusion of another emphatic Cardinals victory, it's starting to look like something large and shiny might be looming over the horizon.

"Winners never cheat, cheaters never win," says Cardinals fan Marty Prather, of Springfield, Mo., who holds up a stuffed tiger before the start of Game 3.

KEY MOMENTS

Jim Edmonds, the only lefthanded batter in the Cardinals lineup, grounded a fourth-inning pitch by lefty Nate Robertson down the right-field line. Albert Pujols and Scott Rolen scored easily for a 2-0 lead.

The double gave Edmonds a team-high 10 RBIs this postseason. Hindered by various ailments, the pending free agent produced only 13 during the regular season's final nine weeks.

"He's got that quality where the bigger the moment, the more likely he's going to concentrate, not get distracted and produce," manager Tony La Russa said. "He's done that ever since he's been here. He really is a prime-time guy."

LEFT: Chris Carpenter is a blur to Tiger hitters all night. He throws only 82 pitches in eight innings, and only 27 of those are out of the strike zone.

GAME 3 FINAL	1	2	3	4	5	6	7	8	9	R	H	E
DETROIT	0	0	0	0	0	0	0	0	0	0	3	1
ST. LOUIS <<	0	0	0	2	0	0	2	1	—	5	7	0

ST. LOUIS CARDINALS

HITTERS	AB	R	H	RBI	BB	SO	AVG
David Eckstein, SS	4	1	2	0	1	0	.154
Preston Wilson, LF	3	1	1	0	2	1	.143
Albert Pujols, 1B	4	1	1	0	0	0	.200
Scott Rolen, 3B	4	1	1	0	1	1	.417
Ronnie Belliard, 2B	4	0	0	0	0	1	.000
Jim Edmonds, CF	2	0	1	2	2	1	.444
Yadier Molina, C	3	0	1	0	1	0	.273
So Taguchi, RF	3	1	0	0	1	1	.143
Chris Carpenter, P	3	0	0	0	0	0	.000
Braden Looper, P	0	0	0	0	0	0	.000
Totals	30	5	7	2	8	5	

PITCHERS	IP	H	R	ER	BB	SO	ERA
Chris Carpenter (W, 1-0)	8.0	3	0	0	0	6	0.00
Braden Looper	1.0	0	0	0	0	0	0.00

BATTING
2B • Pujols (1, Robertson), Edmonds (2, Robertson), Molina (1, Ledezma)
RBI • Edmonds 2 (4)
S • Carpenter
HPB • Pujols (by Miner)
Team LOB • 11

FIELDING
DP • Rolen-Belliard-Pujols

PITCHING
WP • Carpenter
PITCHES-STRIKES • Carpenter 82-55, Looper 11-7
GROUND BALLS-FLY BALLS • Carpenter 12-6, Looper 2-1
BATTERS FACED • Carpenter 26, Looper 3

DETROIT TIGERS

HITTERS	AB	R	H	RBI	BB	SO	AVG
Curtis Granderson, CF	4	0	0	0	0	2	.000
Craig Monroe, LF	4	0	0	0	0	1	.273
Placido Polanco, 2B	3	0	0	0	0	0	.000
Magglio Ordonez, RF	3	0	0	0	0	0	.200
Carlos Guillen, SS	3	0	0	0	0	1	.500
Ivan Rodriguez, C	3	0	0	0	0	1	.000
Sean Casey, 1B	3	0	2	0	0	0	.333
Brandon Inge, 3B	3	0	1	0	0	1	.300
Fernando Rodney, P	0	0	0	0	0	0	.000
Zach Miner, P	0	0	0	0	0	0	.000
Nate Robertson, P	0	0	0	0	0	0	.000
a-Alexis Gomez, PH	1	0	0	0	0	0	.000
Wil Ledezma, P	0	0	0	0	0	0	.000
Joel Zumaya, P	0	0	0	0	0	0	.000
Jason Grilli, P	0	0	0	0	0	0	.000
Neifi Perez, 3B	0	0	0	0	0	0	.000
b-Omar Infante, PH	1	0	0	0	0	0	.000
Totals	28	0	3	0	0	6	

a-popped out for Santiago in the 8th

PITCHERS	IP	H	R	ER	BB	SO	ERA
Nate Robertson (L, 0-1)	5.0	5	2	2	3	3	3.60
Wil Ledezma	0.1	1	0	0	0	1	0.00
Joel Zumaya	1.0	0	2	0	2	1	0.00
Jason Grilli	0.2	0	0	0	1	0	0.00
Fernando Rodney	0.1	1	1	1	2	0	6.75
Zach Miner	0.2	0	0	0	0	0	0.00

BATTING
S • Robertson
Team LOB • 2

FIELDING
DP • Perez-Casey
E • Zumaya (1, throw)

PITCHING
PITCHES-STRIKES • Robertson 93-54, Ledezma 10-5, Zumaya 24-11, Grilli 11-5, Rodney 17-6, Miner 8-5
GROUND BALLS-FLY BALLS • Robertson 3-9, Ledezma 0-0, Zumaya 1-1, Grilli 2-0, Rodney 1-0, Miner 2-0
BATTERS FACED • Robertson 23, Ledezma 2, Zumaya 6, Grilli 3, Rodney 4, Miner 2
INHERITED RUNNERS-SCORED •
Zumaya 1-0, Grilli 1-0, Miner 3-1

Batting and earned-run averages are cumulative for postseason

GAME INFORMATION
Attendance • 46,513
Game time • 3:03
Temperature • 43

UMPIRES
Home • Wally Bell
1st base • Mike Winters
2nd base • John Hirschbeck
3rd base • Tim McClelland
Left field • Randy Marsh
Right field • Alfonso Marquez

HOW THEY SCORED

Cardinals fourth inning • Wilson singled to left and advanced to third on Pujols' double. Rolen walked. Wilson out at home on Belliard's fielder's-choice grounder. Edmonds doubled to right, scoring Pujols and Rolen. • Two runs
Cardinals 2, Tigers 0

Cardinals seventh inning • Eckstein walked. Wilson walked. Pujols grounded to pitcher Zumaya, whose throwing error to third allowed Eckstein and Wilson to score. • Two runs
Cardinals 4, Tigers 0

Cardinals eighth inning • Taguchi walked, took second on Carpenter's sacrifice and third on Eckstein's single. Taguchi scored on Miner's wild pitch. • One run
Final score
Cardinals 5, Tigers 0

SWEET ST. LOUIS

Get your St. Louis Cardinals Championship Package today with your paid subscription to Sports Illustrated

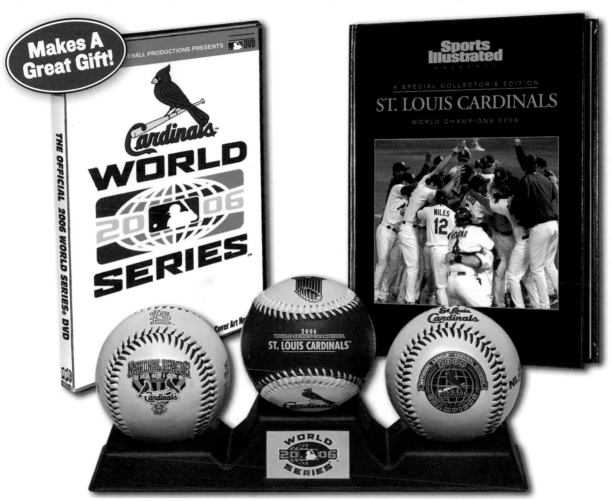

Officially licensed
MLB Productions DVD

Cardinals baseball
set with stand
(FREE when you use your credit card)

SI's hardcover Cardinals
commemorative book

The mighty mite

THE SCENE • BY JOE STRAUSS

Even at its highest level, the game remains a simple one: Catch the ball, then throw it. The Detroit Tigers found each task difficult to solve on a misty Thursday night at Busch Stadium. And because the Cardinals did them well in addition to producing four exquisitely timed two-out hits, an 83-win team stands just one win shy of the franchise's first world title in more than a generation.

A two-run, slip-and-slide seventh inning followed by shortstop David Eckstein's two-out double off the flapping glove of Tigers left fielder Craig Monroe in the eighth provided the difference in a 5-4 win in Game 4 of an increasingly one-sided World Series.

Eckstein, who began the postseason in an eight-for-50 funk, was the centerpiece of both late rallies.

The first received an assist from center fielder Curtis Granderson's slip and Tigers reliever Fernando Rodney's baffling throwing error. The second saw Monroe get a tardy jump on a small man's big hit.

With two out in the eighth, the 5-foot-7 Eckstein turned around Joel Zumaya's high-90s fastball for a line drive that caught Monroe playing too shallow. Trying to retreat, Monroe went horizontal but the ball glanced off his outstretched glove for a double that scored Aaron Miles from second base.

"I was hoping," Eckstein said, "it would find a little bit of grass out there."

When it did, a one-run lead fell to rookie Adam Wainwright, who retired the Tigers in order.

"This is probably the biggest stage you can be on," Eckstein said. "Having the opportunity to be in that situation, I was just hoping I could put a good at-bat together and put the barrel of the bat on the ball. Fortunately I was able to do it."

THE VIEW • BY BRYAN BURWELL

They were dancing in the aisles, making their red-clad bodies gyrate like thousands of uncontrollable spinning tops. They were doing silly little twirls, goofy little hops and foolishly giddy skips between the red seats and cement steps.

With glittering confetti fluttering down from the roof, and red and white fireworks lighting up the misty night sky over sold-out Busch Stadium, 46,000 towel-waving Cardinals fans refused to leave.

They were standing there trying to absorb some kind of miracle that occurred as the Cardinals fought back from a third-inning, 3-0 deficit to beat the Detroit Tigers and win Game 4 by an improbable 5-4 score. They were all trying to absorb the madness of the Redbirds sitting one game from a long overdue World Series championship.

They were laughing and hooting and hollering as they spilled out into the downtown streets. They were blaring their car horns and raising glasses and trying hard not to jinx this thing that is at long last ever so close to fruition.

Are you thinking what I'm thinking?

Shhh, don't say it. At least not yet.

All over St. Louis today, there are giddy loyalists of Cardinal Nation who are convinced they're on the verge of a World Series miracle because of the wild and unpredictable way the Redbirds beat Detroit in Game 4.

It was some kind of baseball miracle, with comebacks that make no sense at all unless you do believe in miracles.

Cardinals shortstop David Eckstein doubles to center, scoring Aaron Miles with the go-ahead run in the eighth inning. Eckstein has four hits, including three doubles.

KEY MOMENTS

Seventh inning, 1968 World Series, Tigers and Cardinals, and Curt Flood slips in center field on a fly ball by Jim Northrup, opening the Flood gates for Detroit's improbable 4-1 victory in Game 7.

Seventh inning, 2006 World Series, Game 4, Tigers and Cardinals, and Detroit's Curtis Granderson slips in center field on a fly ball by David Eckstein. It opened a much smaller gate, but started a Cardinals rally.

The Cardinals trailed 3-2 when Granderson lost his feet in the bottom of the seventh, and Eckstein had a fluke double. The entire mood in Busch Stadium changed after that. As if on cue, So Taguchi's sacrifice bunt was air-mailed into right field by reliever Fernando Rodney for Detroit's sixth error in four games.

Eckstein scrambled home for the tying run. Rodney struck out Jim Edmonds and Scott Rolen, but Preston Wilson made the save by skimming a single into left field, scoring Taguchi for a 4-3 lead.

RIGHT: So Taguchi is safe on Fernando Rodney's throwing error, allowing David Eckstein to score. Tigers second baseman Placido Polanco leaps for the throw.

52

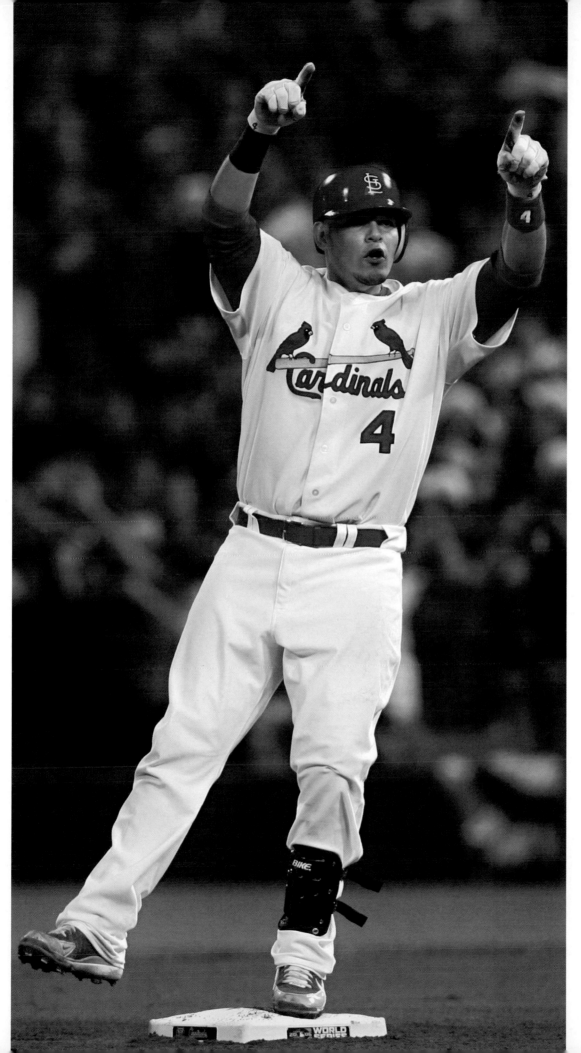

Yadier Molina celebrates after hitting an RBI double to score Scott Rolen in the fourth inning of Game 4.

Tigers left fielder Craig Monroe barely misses a double by David Eckstein that scores Aaron Miles in the eighth. "Eckstein's a little guy," Monroe says after the game. "You don't expect him to hit it that far."

California native Jeff Weaver covers up on a chilly autumn night as his teammates make a Game 4 comeback.

GAME 4 FINAL	1	2	3	4	5	6	7	8	9	R	H	E
DETROIT	0	1	2	0	0	0	0	1	0	4	10	1
ST. LOUIS <<	0	0	1	1	0	0	2	1	—	5	9	0

ST. LOUIS CARDINALS

HITTERS	AB	R	H	RBI	BB	SO	AVG
David Eckstein, SS	5	1	4	2	0	0	.333
Chris Duncan, RF	2	0	0	0	1	0	.167
b-So Taguchi, PH-RF-LF	1	1	0	0	0	0	.125
Albert Pujols, 1B	2	0	0	0	2	1	.167
Jim Edmonds, CF	4	0	0	0	0	3	.308
Scott Rolen, 3B	4	1	2	0	0	1	.438
Preston Wilson, LF	3	0	1	1	0	0	.200
Adam Wainwright, P	0	0	0	0	0	0	.000
Yadier Molina, C	2	0	1	1	2	0	.308
Aaron Miles, 2B	3	2	1	0	1	1	.167
Jeff Suppan, P	2	0	0	0	0	1	.000
a-John Rodriguez, PH	1	0	0	0	0	1	.000
Josh Kinney, P	0	0	0	0	0	0	.000
Tyler Johnson, P	0	0	0	0	0	0	.000
Braden Looper, P	0	0	0	0	0	0	.000
Juan Encarnacion, RF	1	0	0	0	0	1	.000
Totals	**30**	**5**	**9**	**4**	**6**	**9**	

a-Struck out for Suppan in the 6th.
b-Hit a sacrifice bunt for Duncan in the 7th

PITCHERS	IP	H	R	ER	BB	SO	ERA
Jeff Suppan	6.0	8	3	3	2	4	4.50
Josh Kinney	0.2	0	0	0	1	1	0.00
Tyler Johnson	0.1	0	0	0	0	0	0.00
Braden Looper	0.1	1	1	1	0	0	3.86
Adam Wainwright (W, 1-0)	1.2	1	0	0	0	3	0.00

BATTING
2B • Eckstein 3 (3, Bonderman, Rodney, Zumaya), Rolen 2 (3, Bonderman, Bonderman), Molina (2, Bonderman)
RBI • Eckstein 2 (2), Molina (1), Wilson (1)
2-out RBI • Eckstein 2; Molina; Wilson
S • Wilson; Taguchi
HPB • Pujols (by Miner)
Team LOB • 9

BASERUNNING
SB • Miles (1, 2nd base off Bonderman/Rodriguez)

PITCHING
WP • Wainwright
PITCHES-STRIKES • Suppan 87-53, Kinney 13-5, Johnson 1-1, Looper 6-4, Wainwright 23-15
GROUND BALLS-FLY BALLS • Suppan 8-6, Kinney 0-1, Johnson 0-1, Looper 1-0, Wainwright 2-0
BATTERS FACED • Suppan 28, Kinney 3, Johnson 1, Looper 2, Wainwright 6
INHERITED RUNNERS-SCORED • Johnson 1-0, Wainwright 1-1

DETROIT TIGERS

HITTERS	AB	R	H	RBI	BB	SO	AVG
Curtis Granderson, CF	5	1	1	0	0	2	.056
Craig Monroe, LF	5	0	0	0	0	1	.188
Carlos Guillen, SS	3	1	1	0	2	1	.462
Magglio Ordonez, RF	5	0	0	0	0	2	.133
Sean Casey, 1B	4	1	3	2	0	0	.462
Ivan Rodriguez, C	4	1	3	1	0	0	.200
Placido Polanco, 2B	4	0	0	0	0	0	.000
Brandon Inge, 3B	3	0	2	1	1	0	.385
Jeremy Bonderman, P	2	0	0	0	0	1	.000
Fernando Rodney, P	0	0	0	0	0	0	.000
a-Alexis Gomez, PH	1	0	0	0	0	1	.000
Joel Zumaya, P	0	0	0	0	0	0	.000
Totals	**36**	**4**	**10**	**4**	**3**	**8**	

a-Struck out for Rodney in the 8th

PITCHERS	IP	H	R	ER	BB	SO	ERA
Jeremy Bonderman	5.1	6	2	2	4	4	3.38
Fernando Rodney	1.2	2	2	0	1	4	3.00
Joel Zumaya (L, 0-1)	1.0	1	1	1	1	1	4.50

Batting and earned-run averages are cumulative for postseason

BATTING
2B • Granderson (1, Suppan), Rodriguez (1, Looper), Inge (1, Wainwright)
HR • Casey (1)
RBI • Casey 2 (3), Rodriguez (1), Inge (1)
2-out RBI • Casey; Rodriguez
S • Bonderman
Team LOB • 9

BASERUNNING
SB • Guillen (1, 2nd base off Kinney/Molina)

FIELDING
E • Rodney (1, throw)
DP • Guillen-Casey
Outfield assists • Monroe (Pujols at 3rd base)

PITCHING
PITCHES-STRIKES • Bonderman 92-59, Rodney 30-17, Zumaya 19-9
GROUND BALLS-FLY BALLS •
Bonderman 11-1, Rodney 0-0, Zumaya 1-1
BATTERS FACED • Bonderman 25, Rodney 8, Zumaya 5
INHERITED RUNNERS-SCORED • Rodney 2-0

GAME INFORMATION
Attendance • 46,470
Game time • 3:35
Temperature • 53

UMPIRES
Home • Mike Winters
1st base • John Hirschbeck
2nd base • Tim McClelland
3rd base • Randy Marsh
Left field • Alfonso Marquez
Right field • Wally Bell

HOW THEY SCORED
Tigers second inning •
Casey homered to right with one out • One run
Tigers 1, Cardinals 0

Tigers third inning •
Granderson doubled to right. WIth one out, Guillen walked. With two outs, Casey singled to right, scoring Granderson and moving Guillen to third. Rodriguez singled to right, scoring Guillen • Two runs
Tigers 3, Cardinals 0

Cardinals third inning •
With one out, Miles singled and stole second. With two outs, Eckstein doubled to center, scoring Miles • One run
Tigers 3, Cardinals 1

Cardinals fourth inning •
With one out, Rolen doubled to left and went to third on Wilson's ground-out. Molina doubled to left, scoring Rolen • One run
Tigers 3, Cardinals 2

Cardinals seventh inning •
Eckstein doubled to center and scored when Taguchi was safe at second on a sacrifice bunt and pitcher Rodney's throwing error. Pujols was intentionally walked. With two outs, Wilson singled to left, scoring Taguchi • Two runs
Cardinals 4, Tigers 3

Tigers eighth inning •
Rodriguez doubled to left and went to third on Polanco's groundout. Inge doubled to center, scoring Rodriguez • One run
Cardinals 4, Tigers 4

Cardinals eighth inning •
Molina walked. Miles reached on fielder's choice, Molina out at second. Miles went to second on Zumaya's wild pitch. With two outs, Eckstein doubled to center, scoring Miles • One run
Final score
Cardinals 5, Tigers 4

Here's to America's national pastime.

And to baseball.

The Official Soft Drink of the St. Louis Cardinals since 1966

A perfect 10

THE SCENE • BY JOE STRAUSS

Dancing then falling as a group before a crowd of 46,638, the Cardinals, a team seemingly splitting at its seams weeks ago, celebrated the redemptive power of October more than any team before them.

The first team to baptize a new ballpark with a World Series championship since 1923, the Cardinals won their first Series title since 1982 by completing a five-game domination of the Detroit Tigers with a 4-2 validation at Busch Stadium.

Starting pitcher Jeff Weaver, a July acquisition deemed not good enough by the Los Angeles Angels, offered a nerveless performance to further belie his reputation as a weak-kneed autumn arm.

Shortstop David Eckstein ended a World Series that began with 11 hitless at-bats by accounting for his team's first two RBIs in Game 5 and acknowledgement as Series MVP.

"We did not stay in the past, and we weren't looking toward the future. We stayed in the moment," said Eckstein, who finished with a .364 overall average to go with six hits and four RBIs in the Series' final two games.

A bullpen thought destitute after the Sept. 7 loss of closer Jason Isringhausen again provided the final punctuation point, this time with rookie Adam Wainwright finishing it by overpowering Tigers third baseman Brandon Inge on a three-pitch strikeout.

The Cardinals didn't just win their 10th World Series. They emerged from a disconsolate 83-win season, a 12-17 September and a near-calamitous final two weeks to outdo the 85-win 1987 Minnesota Twins for translating the fewest regular-season victories into a championship.

"We shocked the world," Jim Edmonds said.

"We tasted a lot of failure this season," third baseman Scott Rolen said. "I can tell you this tastes a lot better."

THE VIEW • BY BERNIE MIKLASZ

The 10th World Series championship in Cardinals history was for all the Cardinals teams of the past that played special baseball all summer, only to come up short, staggering off into the winter, filled with frustration and longing.

This was to give peace to all of the postseason ghosts and to soften the haunted memories, whether it's Curt Flood's slip in 1968, or umpire Don Denkinger's blown call at first base in 1985.

This was for the franchise immortals who always return home, a college of Cardinals, visiting this baseball Vatican in St. Louis. They are living monuments: Stan Musial, Bob Gibson, Lou Brock, Ozzie Smith, Red Schoendienst and Bruce Sutter. Their presence reminds new generations of Cardinals that theirs is an extraordinary legacy, always to be handled with care.

This was for old friends who could not be there, but you just know that the spirits of Jack Buck and Darryl Kile were close to the Cardinals and their fans, watching over the drama of Game 5.

This was for baseball's best fans, who had waited 23 seasons for a reaffirmation of the proud franchise's glorious tradition. It doesn't matter where they were gathered for Game 5. They could have been shivering in the frigid bowl of Busch Stadium, or watching by the fireplace at home, or bonding with friends in a local sports bar, or watching on satellite from a base camp in Iraq, or an outpost in Afghanistan.

Cardinals fans live everywhere, existing as one extended family, and they became one nation under a groove again on Oct. 27, when the power of this Red October pulled their heartbeats together in an electric moment. At 10:26 in the evening, rookie Cardinals closer Adam Wainwright struck out the Tigers' Brandon Inge on a heinous breaking ball, sealing World Series title No. 10.

For the first pitch of Game 5, the Cardinals bring out No. 6. Stan "The Man" Musial demonstrates that his swing is just as sweet as ever.

ABOVE: A broken bat doesn't keep David Eckstein from singling in Yadier Molina with the first run in Game 5.
RIGHT: Ivan Rodriguez grimaces and Yadier Molina grins after Molina scores on a throwing error by Justin Verlander in the
fourth inning.

KEY MOMENTS

With the Cardinals trailing 2-1 in the bottom of the fourth, consecutive one-out singles by Yadier Molina and So Taguchi created an obvious bunt situation for Jeff Weaver. The pitcher's bunt was too hard and directly at Tigers starter Justin Verlander. Rather than go to second base to start a double play, Verlander threw after the lead runner at third.

His throw sailed wide, allowing Molina to score and Taguchi to take third base. From there, Taguchi scored the inning's second unearned run — and the eighth of the series — on Eckstein's groundball as the Cardinals reclaimed the lead 3-2.

Detroit pitchers committed an error in all five World Series games, with Verlander the guilty party in Game 1, also.

RIGHT: After fanning Brandon Inge for the final out in Game 5, Cards closer Adam Wainwright lets out a victory yell as the celebration begins.

ABOVE: Closer Adam Wainwright and catcher Yadier Molina jump for joy as Game 5 ends and the revelry starts.
NEXT PAGE: The Cardinals gather en masse for the ultimate group hug after winning the World Series.

Shortstop David Eckstein, the Series MVP, launches himself into supersub Scott Spiezio's arms in the Game 5 aftermath.

As fireworks erupt and the crowd goes crazy, folks, the Cardinals swarm over the infield.

Cardinals fans whoop it up after watching the Redbirds dispatch Detroit in Game 5 and capture the team's 10th World Series championship.

With his son, A.J., along for the ride, Albert Pujols watches Cardinals chairman Bill DeWitt Jr. accept the World Series championship trophy.

Tears of joy flow from the eyes of Lori Zey of Manchester, Mo., as she watches the Cardinals celebrate winning the World Series in Busch Stadium.

Streamers fill the air as the Cardinals stream onto the Busch Stadium infield after winning Game 5.

Jeremy Mizeur (left) of Springfield, Ill., adds vocal support to the din that ensues when the crowd celebrates after the last out.

With Game 5 over, Tony La Russa shows his exuberance after managing a team to a World Series championship for the second time in his career. His wife, Elaine, joins the celebration.

Outfielder So Taguchi gives new meaning to the term "all smiles" as he tosses batting gloves to fans in the stands and makes his way around the field.

Center fielder Jim Edmonds takes time out from the post-Game 5 melee to have some face-time with family members.

Loud hollering and wild gesturing abound as the fans packing Busch Stadium voice their pleasure after the Cardinals' victory.

78

Fans give Jeff
Weaver, the winning
pitcher in Game 5,
their approval with
a show of hands as
he celebrates the
victory by high-
fiving everyone
within reach.

Third baseman Scott Rolen makes his way through a throng of celebrating fans as he accepts congratulations for the Cardinals' victory.

Wearing goggles to shield his eyes from a fizzy shower, pitcher Chris Carpenter (right) contributes to the dousing going on during the post-Game 5 celebration.

Yadier Molina adds to the abundance of liquid being sprayed as the jubilant Cardinals uncork both bubbly and emotions.

World Series MVP David Eckstein is the center of attention for both cameramen and teammates, with the latter enjoying giving him a champagne shower.

Chris Duncan, the starting right fielder in Game 5, makes sure his father, pitching coach Dave Duncan, doesn't avoid a good soaking.

Pumped-up fans salute the Cardinals as the victory celebration spills out of Busch Stadium and into surrounding streets.

Cardinals fans survey the celebration from their perch on the Stan Musial statue in front of Busch Stadium.

Washington University students James Mosbacher (left) and Anchit Mehrotra are not shy in expressing their exhilaration about the Cardinals' victory in Game 5.

	1	2	3	4	5	6	7	8	9	R	H	E
DETROIT	0	0	0	2	0	0	0	0	0	2	5	2
ST. LOUIS <<	0	1	0	2	0	0	1	0	—	4	8	1

ST. LOUIS CARDINALS

HITTERS	AB	R	H	RBI	BB	SO	AVG
David Eckstein, SS	4	1	2	2	0	0	.364
Chris Duncan, RF	2	0	0	0	1	1	.125
Preston Wilson, LF	0	0	0	0	1	0	.200
Albert Pujols, 1B	3	0	1	0	1	1	.200
Jim Edmonds, CF	4	0	0	0	0	1	.235
Scott Rolen, 3B	3	0	1	1	1	0	.421
Ronnie Belliard, 2B	4	0	0	0	0	1	.000
Yadier Molina, C	4	2	3	0	0	0	.412
So Taguchi, LF-RF	3	1	1	0	0	1	.182
Jeff Weaver, P	3	0	0	0	0	0	.000
a-Scott Spiezio, PH	1	0	0	0	0	0	.000
Adam Wainwright, P	0	0	0	0	0	0	.000
Totals	**31**	**4**	**8**	**3**	**4**	**5**	

a-Popped out for Weaver in the 8th.

PITCHERS	IP	H	R	ER	BB	SO	ERA
Weaver (W, 1-1)	8.0	4	2	1	1	9	2.77
Wainwright (S, 1)	1.0	1	0	0	1	1	0.00

BATTING
RBI • Eckstein 2 (4), Rolen (2)
2-out RBI • Eckstein; Rolen
S • Taguchi
Team LOB • 8

BASERUNNING
CS • Pujols (1, 2nd base by Verlander/Rodriguez)

FIELDING
E • Duncan (1, fielding)

PITCHING
WP • Weaver
PITCHES-STRIKES • Weaver 99-69, Wainwright 26-14
GROUND BALLS-FLY BALLS • Weaver 9-6, Wainwright 2-0
BATTERS FACED • Weaver 30, Wainwright 5

DETROIT TIGERS

HITTERS	AB	R	H	RBI	BB	SO	AVG
Curtis Granderson, CF	3	0	1	0	1	1	.095
Craig Monroe, LF	4	0	0	0	0	2	.150
Joel Zumaya, P	0	0	0	0	0	0	.000
Carlos Guillen, SS	4	0	0	0	0	1	.353
Magglio Ordonez, RF	4	1	0	0	0	1	.105
Sean Casey, 1B	4	1	3	2	0	1	.529
1-Ramon Santiago, PR	0	0	0	0	0	0	.200
Ivan Rodriguez, C	4	0	0	0	0	1	.158
Placido Polanco, 2B	3	0	0	0	1	0	.000
Brandon Inge, 3B	4	0	1	0	0	2	.353
Justin Verlander, P	2	0	0	0	0	1	.000
a-Alexis Gomez, PH	1	0	0	0	0	0	.000
Fernando Rodney, P	0	0	0	0	0	0	.000
Marcus Thames, LF	0	0	0	0	0	0	.000
Totals	**33**	**2**	**5**	**2**	**2**	**10**	

a-Flied out for Verlander in the 7th.
1-Ran for Casey in the 9th.

PITCHERS	IP	H	R	ER	BB	SO	ERA
Justin Verlander (L, 0-2)	6.0	6	3	1	3	4	5.73
Fernando Rodney	1.0	2	1	1	1	0	4.50
Joel Zumaya	1.0	0	0	0	0	1	3.00

BATTING
2B • Inge (2, Weaver), Casey 2 (2, Weaver, Wainwright)
HR • Casey (2, 4th inning off Weaver, 1 on, 1 out)
RBI • Casey 2 (5)
Team LOB • 6

FIELDING
E • Inge (3, throw), Verlander (2, throw)
DP • (Rodriguez-Guillen-Casey)

PITCHING
PITCHES-STRIKES • Verlander 101-58, Rodney 25-14, Zumaya 6-5
GROUND BALLS-FLY BALLS • Verlander 7-6, Rodney 1-2, Zumaya 0-2
BATTERS FACED • Verlander 27, Rodney 6, Zumaya 3

Batting and earned-run averages are cumulative for postseason

HOW THEY SCORED

Cardinals second inning • Molina singled, went to second on Taguchi's sacrifice and to third on Weaver's groundout. Eckstein singled, scoring Molina • One run
Cardinals 1, Tigers 0

Tigers fourth inning • With one out, Ordonez reached second on right fielder Duncan's error. Casey followed with a homer to right • Two runs
Tigers 2, Cardinals 1

Cardinals fourth inning • With one out, Molina singled and Taguchi singled. Weaver bunted, and pitcher Verlander's wild throw to third scored Molina. Taguchi advanced to third and scored on Eckstein's groundout • Two runs
Cardinals 3, Tigers 2

Cardinals seventh inning • Eckstein singled. Wilson walked. With two outs, Rolen singled to right, scoring Eckstein • One run
**Final score
Cardinals 4, Tigers 2**

GAME INFORMATION
Attendance • 46,638
Game time • 2:56
Temperature • 47

UMPIRES
Home • John Hirschbeck
1st base • Tim McClelland
2nd base • Randy Marsh
3rd base • Alfonso Marquez
Left field • Wally Bell
Right field • Mike Winters

Joe Plumley of St. Louis lugs a stuffed tiger that symbolizes the vanquished Detroit Tigers as he celebrates outside Busch Stadium.

CREDITS

Cover photo by Laurie Skrivan on Oct. 27, 2006.

General manager Walt Jocketty and manager Tony La Russa enjoy a victory dance.